Key Facts™ on

Ireland

~Essential Information on Ireland~

By Patrick W. Nee

The Internationalist®
www.internationalist.com

The Internationalist®

International Business, Investment, and Travel

Published by:

The Internationalist Publishing Company

96 Walter Street/ Suite 200

Boston, MA 02131, USA

Tel: 617-354-7722

www.internationalist.com

PN@internationalist.com

Copyright © 2013 by PWN

The Internationalist is a Registered Trademark. "Key Facts" and "The Internationalist Business Guides" are Trademarks of The Internationalist Publishing Company.

All Rights are reserved under International, Pan-American, and Pan-Asian Conventions. No part of this book may be reproduced in any form without the written permission of the publisher. All rights vigorously enforced

Table Of Contents

Chapter 1: Background

Chapter 2: Geography

Chapter 3: People and Society

Chapter 4: Government and Key Leaders

Chapter 5: Economy

Chapter 6: Energy

Chapter 7: Communications

Chapter 8: Transportation

Chapter 9: Military

Chapter 10: Transnational Issues

Map of Ireland

Chapter 1: Background

Celtic tribes arrived on the island between 600 and 150 B.C. Invasions by Norsemen that began in the late 8th century were finally ended when King Brian BORU defeated the Danes in 1014. English invasions began in the 12th century and set off more than seven centuries of Anglo-Irish struggle marked by fierce rebellions and harsh repressions. A failed 1916 Easter Monday Rebellion touched off several years of guerrilla warfare that in 1921 resulted in independence from the UK for 26 southern counties; six northern (Ulster) counties remained part of the UK. In 1949, Ireland withdrew from the British Commonwealth; it joined the European Community in 1973. Irish governments have sought the peaceful unification of Ireland and have cooperated with Britain against terrorist groups. A peace settlement for Northern Ireland is gradually being implemented despite some difficulties. In 2006, the Irish and British governments developed and began to implement the St. Andrews Agreement, building on the Good Friday Agreement approved in 1998.

Chapter 2: Geography

Location:
Western Europe, occupying five-sixths of the island of Ireland in the North Atlantic Ocean, west of Great Britain

Geographic coordinates:
53 00 N, 8 00 W

Map references:
Europe

Area:
total: 70,273 sq km
country comparison to the world: 120
land: 68,883 sq km
water: 1,390 sq km

Area - comparative:
slightly larger than West Virginia

Land boundaries:
total: 360 km
border countries: UK 360 km

Coastline:
1,448 km

Maritime claims:
territorial sea: 12 nm
exclusive fishing zone: 200 nm

Climate:
temperate maritime; modified by North Atlantic Current; mild winters, cool summers; consistently humid; overcast about half the time

Terrain:
mostly level to rolling interior plain surrounded by rugged hills and low mountains; sea cliffs on west coast

Elevation extremes:

lowest point: Atlantic Ocean 0 m

highest point: Carrauntoohil 1,041 m

Natural resources:

natural gas, peat, copper, lead, zinc, silver, barite, gypsum, limestone, dolomite

Land use:

arable land: 15.11%

permanent crops: 0.01%

other: 84.87% (2011)

Irrigated land:

11 sq km (2003)

Total renewable water resources:

52 cu km (2011)

Freshwater withdrawal (domestic/industrial/agricultural):

total: 0.79 cu km/yr (94%/6%/0%)

per capita: 226.9 cu m/yr (2007)

Natural hazards:

NA

Environment - current issues:

water pollution, especially of lakes, from agricultural runoff

Environment - international agreements:

party to: Air Pollution, Air Pollution-Nitrogen Oxides, Air Pollution-Sulfur 94, Biodiversity, Climate Change, Climate Change-Kyoto Protocol, Desertification, Endangered Species, Environmental Modification, Hazardous Wastes, Law of the Sea, Marine Dumping, Ozone Layer Protection, Ship Pollution, Tropical Timber 83, Tropical Timber 94, Wetlands, Whaling

signed, but not ratified: Air Pollution-Persistent Organic Pollutants, Marine Life Conservation

Geography - note:

strategic location on major air and sea routes between North America and northern Europe; over 40% of the population resides within 100 km of Dublin

Chapter 3: People and Society

Nationality:

noun: Irishman(men), Irishwoman(women), Irish (collective plural)

adjective: Irish

Ethnic groups:

Irish 87.4%, other white 7.5%, Asian 1.3%, black 1.1%, mixed 1.1%, unspecified 1.6% (2006 census)

Languages:

English (official, the language generally used), Irish (Gaelic or Gaeilge) (official, spoken mainly in areas along the western coast)

Religions:

Roman Catholic 87.4%, Church of Ireland 2.9%, other Christian 1.9%, other 2.1%, unspecified 1.5%, none 4.2% (2006 census)

Population:

4,775,982 (July 2013 est.)

country comparison to the world: 119

Age structure:

0-14 years: 21.4% (male 521,145/female 499,367)

15-24 years: 12% (male 291,090/female 282,364)

25-54 years: 44.4% (male 1,065,685/female 1,055,339)

55-64 years: 10.1% (male 241,918/female 240,193)

65 years and over: 12.1% (male 265,533/female 313,348) (2013 est.)

Median age:

total: 35.4 years

male: 35.1 years

female: 35.8 years (2013 est.)

Population growth rate:

1.16% (2013 est.)

country comparison to the world: 99

Birth rate:

15.5 births/1,000 population (2013 est.)

country comparison to the world: 130

Death rate:

6.41 deaths/1,000 population (2013 est.)

country comparison to the world: 152

Net migration rate:

2.51 migrant(s)/1,000 population (2013 est.)

country comparison to the world: 33

Urbanization:

urban population: 62% of total population (2010)

rate of urbanization: 1.8% annual rate of change (2010-15 est.)

Major urban areas - population:

DUBLIN (capital) 1.084 million (2009)

Sex ratio:

at birth: 1.06 male(s)/female

0-14 years: 1.04 male(s)/female

15-24 years: 1.03 male(s)/female

25-54 years: 1.01 male(s)/female

55-64 years: 1.01 male(s)/female

65 years and over: 0.84 male(s)/female

total population: 1 male(s)/female (2013 est.)

Maternal mortality rate:

6 deaths/100,000 live births (2010)

country comparison to the world: 169

Infant mortality rate:

total: 3.78 deaths/1,000 live births

country comparison to the world: 203

male: 4.16 deaths/1,000 live births

female: 3.38 deaths/1,000 live births (2013 est.)

Life expectancy at birth:

total population: 80.44 years

country comparison to the world: 26
male: 78.18 years
female: 82.83 years (2013 est.)

Total fertility rate:
2.01 children born/woman (2013 est.)
country comparison to the world: 128

Contraceptive prevalence rate:
64.8%
note: percent of women aged 18-49 (2004/05)

Health expenditures:
9.2% of GDP (2010)
country comparison to the world: 39

Physicians density:
3.19 physicians/1,000 population (2008)

Hospital bed density:
4.9 beds/1,000 population (2008)

Drinking water source:
improved:
urban: 100% of population
rural: 100% of population
total: 100% of population (2010 est.)

Sanitation facility access:
improved:
urban: 100% of population
rural: 98% of population
total: 99% of population
unimproved:
urban: 0% of population
rural: 2% of population
total: 1% of population (2010 est.)

HIV/AIDS - adult prevalence rate:

0.2% (2009 est.)

country comparison to the world: 101

HIV/AIDS - people living with HIV/AIDS:

6,900 (2009 est.)

country comparison to the world: 113

HIV/AIDS - deaths:

fewer than 100 (2009 est.)

country comparison to the world: 118

Obesity - adult prevalence rate:

25.2% (2008)

country comparison to the world: 57

Education expenditures:

6.5% of GDP (2009)

country comparison to the world: 30

Literacy:

definition: age 15 and over can read and write

total population: 99%

male: 99%

female: 99% (2003 est.)

School life expectancy (primary to tertiary education):

total: 19 years

male: 19 years

female: 19 years (2011)

Unemployment, youth ages 15-24:

total: 29.4%

country comparison to the world: 27

male: 35.3%

female: 23.3% (2011)

Mother's mean age at first birth:

29.8 (2011 est.)

Chapter 4: Government and Key Leaders

Country name:

conventional long form: none

conventional short form: Ireland

local long form: none

local short form: Eire

Government type:

republic, parliamentary democracy

Capital:

name: Dublin

geographic coordinates: 53 19 N, 6 14 W

time difference: UTC 0 (5 hours ahead of Washington, DC during Standard Time)

daylight saving time: +1hr, begins last Sunday in March; ends last Sunday in October

Administrative divisions:

29 counties and 5 cities*; Carlow, Cavan, Clare, Cork, Cork*, Donegal, Dublin*, Dun Laoghaire-Rathdown, Fingal, Galway, Galway*, Kerry, Kildare, Kilkenny, Laois, Leitrim, Limerick, Limerick*, Longford, Louth, Mayo, Meath, Monaghan, North Tipperary, Offaly, Roscommon, Sligo, South Dublin, South Tipperary, Waterford, Waterford*, Westmeath, Wexford, Wicklow

Independence:

6 December 1921 (from the UK by treaty)

National holiday:

Saint Patrick's Day, 17 March

Constitution:

adopted 1 July 1937 by plebiscite; effective 29 December 1937

Legal system:

common law system based on the English model but substantially modified by customary law; judicial review of legislative acts in Supreme Court

International law organization participation:

has not submitted an ICJ jurisdiction declaration; accepts ICCt jurisdiction

Suffrage:
> 18 years of age; universal

Executive branch:
> chief of state: President Michael D. HIGGINS (since 29 October 2011)
> head of government: Taoiseach (Prime Minister) Enda KENNY (since 9 March 2011)
> cabinet: Cabinet appointed by the president with previous nomination by the prime minister and approval of the lower house of Parliament
> elections: president elected by popular vote for a seven-year term (eligible for a second term); election last held on 29 October 2011 (next to be held in October 2018); taoiseach (prime minister} nominated by the House of Representatives (Dail Eireann) and appointed by the president
> election results: Michael D. HIGGINS elected president; percent of vote - Michael D. HIGGINS 39.6%, Sean GALLAGHER 28.5%, Martin MCGUINNESS 13.7%, Gay MITCHELL 6.4%, David NORRIS 6.2%, other 5.6%

Legislative branch:
> bicameral Parliament or Oireachtas consists of the Senate or Seanad Eireann (60 seats; 49 members elected by the universities and from candidates put forward by five vocational panels, 11 are nominated by the prime minister; members serve five-year terms) and the lower house of Parliament or Dail Eireann (166 seats; members elected by popular vote on the basis of proportional representation to serve five-year terms)
> elections: Senate - last held in 27 April 2011 (next to be held 2016); House of Representatives - last held on 25 February 2011 (next to be held probably in 2016)
> election results: Senate - percent of vote by party - NA; seats by party - Fine Gael 19, Fianna Fail 14, Labor Party 12, Sinn Fein 3, independents 12; House of Representatives - percent of vote by party - Fine Gael 45.8%, Labor Party 22.3%, Fianna Fail 12.0%, Sinn Fein 8.4%, United Left Alliance 3.0%, New Vision 0.6%, independents 7.8%; seats by party - Fine Gael 76, Labor Party 37, Fianna Fail 20, Sinn Fein 14, United Left Alliance 5, New Vision 1, independents 13; note - after November 2009 disbandment of the Progressive Democrats, the two members of the Senate continued as independent DPs
> note: on 8 November 2008, delegates voted to disband the Progressive Democrats, and in November 2009 it officially stopped operating as a political party

Judicial branch:
    <u>highest court(s)</u>: Supreme Court or Court of Final Appeal (consists of the chief justice and 7 judges)
    <u>judge selection and term of office</u>: judges nominated by the prime minister and Cabinet and appointed by the president; judges serve till age 70
    <u>subordinate courts</u>: High Court, Court of Criminal Appeal; circuit and district courts

Political parties and leaders:
    Fianna Fail [Michael MARTIN]
    Fine Gael [Enda KENNY]
    Green Party [Eamon RYAN]
    Labor Party [Eamon GILMORE]
    New Vision
    Sinn Fein [Gerry ADAMS]
    Socialist Party [Joe HIGGINS]
    The Workers' Party [Michael FINNEGAN]
    United Left Alliance

Political pressure groups and leaders:
    Families Acting for Innocent Relatives or FAIR [Brian MCCONNELL] (seek compensation for victims of violence);
    Families Against Intimidation and Terror or FAIT (oppose terrorism);
    Gaeltacht Civil Rights Campaign (Coiste Cearta Sibhialta na Gaeilge) or CCSG (encourages the use of the Irish language and campaigns for greater civil rights in Irish speaking areas);
    Iona Institute [David QUINN] (a conservative Catholic think tank);
    Irish Anti-War Movement [Richard BOYD BARRETT] (campaigns against wars around the world);
    Irish Republican Army or IRA (terrorist group);
    Keep Ireland Open (environmental group);
    Midland Railway Action Group or MRAG [Willie ALLEN] (transportation promoters);
    Peace and Neutrality Alliance [Roger COLE] (campaigns to protect Irish neutrality);
    Rail Users Ireland (formerly the Platform 11 - transportation promoters);

32 Country Sovereignty Movement or 32CSM (supports a fully sovereign Ireland); Ulster Defence Association or UDA (terrorist group)

International organization participation:

ADB (nonregional member), Australia Group, BIS, CD, CE, EAPC, EBRD, ECB, EIB, EMU, ESA, EU, FAO, FATF, IAEA, IBRD, ICAO, ICC (national committees), ICRM, IDA, IEA, IFAD, IFC, IFRCS, IGAD (partners), IHO, ILO, IMF, IMO, Interpol, IOC, IOM, IPU, ISO, ITSO, ITU, ITUC (NGOs), MIGA, MINURSO, MONUSCO, NEA, NSG, OAS (observer), OECD, OPCW, OSCE, Paris Club, PCA, PFP, UN, UNCTAD, UNESCO, UNHCR, UNIDO, UNIFIL, UNITAR, UNOCI, UNRWA, UNTSO, UPU, WCO, WHO, WIPO, WMO, WTO, ZC

Diplomatic representation in the US:

chief of mission: Ambassador Michael COLLINS

chancery: 2234 Massachusetts Avenue NW, Washington, DC 20008

telephone: [1] (202) 462-3939

FAX: [1] (202) 232-5993

consulate(s) general: Atlanta, Boston, Chicago, New York, San Francisco

Diplomatic representation from the US:

chief of mission: Ambassador (vacant); Charge d'Affaires John HENNESSEY-NILAND

embassy: 42 Elgin Road, Ballsbridge, Dublin 4

mailing address: use embassy street address

telephone: [353] (1) 668-8777

FAX: [353] (1) 668-9946

Key Leaders:

Pres.	Michael Daniel HIGGINS
Taoiseach (Prime Min.)	Enda KENNY
Dep. Prime Min.	Eamon GILMORE
Min. for Agriculture, Food, & the Marine	Simon COVENEY

Min. for Arts, Heritage, & Gaeltacht Affairs	Jimmy DEENIHAN
Min. for Children	Frances FITZGERALD
Min. for Communications, Energy, & Natural Resources	Pat RABBITTE
Min. for Defense	Alan Joseph SHATTER
Min. for Education & Skills	Ruairi QUINN
Min. for Enterprise, Jobs, & Innovation	Richard BRUTON
Min. for Environment, Community, & Local Govt.	Phil HOGAN
Min. for Finance	Michael NOONAN
Min. for Foreign Affairs & Trade	Eamon GILMORE
Min. for Health	James REILLY
Min. for Justice & Equality	Alan Joseph SHATTER
Min. for Public Expenditure & Reform	Brendan HOWLIN
Min. for Social Protection	Joan BURTON
Min. for Transport,	Leo VARADKAR

Tourism, & Sport	
Attorney Gen.	Maire WHELAN
Governor, Central Bank of Ireland	Patrick HONOHAN
Ambassador to the US	Michael COLLINS
Permanent Representative to the UN, New York	Anne Colette ANDERSON

Flag description:

three equal vertical bands of green (hoist side), white, and orange; officially the flag colors have no meaning, but a common interpretation is that the green represents the Irish nationalist (Gaelic) tradition of Ireland; orange represents the Orange tradition (minority supporters of William of Orange); white symbolizes peace (or a lasting truce) between the green and the orange

note: similar to the flag of Cote d'Ivoire, which is shorter and has the colors reversed - orange (hoist side), white, and green; also similar to the flag of Italy, which is shorter and has colors of green (hoist side), white, and red

National symbol(s):

harp

National anthem:

name: "Amhran na bhFiann" (The Soldier's Song)

lyrics/music: Peadar KEARNEY [English], Liam O RINN [Irish]/Patrick HEENEY and Peadar KEARNEY

note: adopted 1926; instead of "Amhran na bhFiann," the song "Ireland's Call" is often used in athletic events where citizens of the Republic of Ireland and Northern Ireland compete as a unified team

Chapter 5: Economy

Economy - overview:

Ireland is a small, modern, trade-dependent economy. Ireland was among the initial group of 12 EU nations that began circulating the euro on 1 January 2002. GDP growth averaged 6% in 1995-2007, but economic activity has dropped sharply since the onset of the world financial crisis, with GDP falling by over 3% in 2008, nearly 7% in 2009, and less than 1% in 2010. Ireland entered into a recession in 2008 for the first time in more than a decade, with the subsequent collapse of its domestic property and construction markets. Property prices rose more rapidly in Ireland in the decade up to 2007 than in any other developed economy. Since their 2007 peak, average house prices have fallen 47%. In the wake of the collapse of the construction sector and the downturn in consumer spending and business investment, the export sector, dominated by foreign multinationals, has become a key component of Ireland's economy. Agriculture, once the most important sector, is now dwarfed by industry and services. In 2008 the former COWEN government moved to guarantee all bank deposits, recapitalize the banking system, and establish partly-public venture capital funds in response to the country's economic downturn. In 2009, in continued efforts to stabilize the banking sector, the Irish Government established the National Asset Management Agency (NAMA) to acquire problem commercial property and development loans from Irish banks. Faced with sharply reduced revenues and a burgeoning budget deficit, the Irish Government introduced the first in a series of draconian budgets in 2009. In addition to across-the-board cuts in spending, the 2009 budget included wage reductions for all public servants. These measures were not sufficient. In 2010, the budget deficit reached 32.4% of GDP - the world's largest deficit, as a percentage of GDP - because of additional government support for the banking sector. In late 2010, the former COWEN government agreed to a $112 billion loan package from the EU and IMF to help Dublin further increase the capitalization of its banking sector and avoid defaulting on its sovereign debt. Since entering office in March 2011, the new KENNY government has intensified austerity measures to try to meet the deficit targets under Ireland's EU-IMF program. Ireland achieved moderate growth of 1.4% in 2011 and cut the budget deficit to 9.1% of GDP.

Although the recovery slowed in 2012 because of weaker EU demand for Irish exports, Dublin managed to trim the deficit to about 8.5% of GDP.

GDP (purchasing power parity):
$195.4 billion (2012 est.)
country comparison to the world: 58
$193.6 billion (2011 est.)
$190.8 billion (2010 est.)
note: data are in 2012 US dollars

GDP (official exchange rate):
$210.4 billion (2012 est.)

GDP - real growth rate:
0.9% (2012 est.)
country comparison to the world: 163
1.4% (2011 est.)
-0.8% (2010 est.)

GDP - per capita (PPP):
$42,600 (2012 est.)
country comparison to the world: 24
$42,300 (2011 est.)
$41,900 (2010 est.)
note: data are in 2012 US dollars

GDP - composition by sector:
agriculture: 1.8%
industry: 26.3%
services: 72% (2012 est.)

Labor force:
2.154 million (2012 est.)
country comparison to the world: 120

Labor force - by occupation:
agriculture: 5%
industry: 19%

services: 76% (2011 est.)

Unemployment rate:

14.7% (2012 est.)

country comparison to the world: 142

14.4% (2011 est.)

Population below poverty line:

5.5% (2009)

Household income or consumption by percentage share:

lowest 10%: 2.9%

highest 10%: 27.2% (2000)

Distribution of family income - Gini index:

33.9 (2010)

country comparison to the world: 94

35.9 (1987)

Investment (gross fixed):

10% of GDP (2012 est.)

country comparison to the world: 150

Budget:

revenues: $72.76 billion

expenditures: $88.49 billion (2012 est.)

Taxes and other revenues:

34.6% of GDP (2012 est.)

country comparison to the world: 67

Budget surplus (+) or deficit (-):

-7.5% of GDP (2012 est.)

country comparison to the world: 190

Public debt:

118.4% of GDP (2012 est.)

country comparison to the world: 10

106.4% of GDP (2011 est.)

note: data cover general government debt, and includes debt instruments issued (or owned) by government entities other than the treasury; the data include treasury debt held by foreign entities; the data include debt issued by subnational entities, as well as intra-governmental debt; intra-governmental debt consists of treasury borrowings from surpluses in the social funds, such as for retirement, medical care, and unemployment; debt instruments for the social funds are not sold at public auctions

Inflation rate (consumer prices):

1.7% (2012 est.)

country comparison to the world: 31

2.6% (2011 est.)

Central bank discount rate:

1.5% (31 December 2012)

country comparison to the world: 118

1.75% (31 December 2010)

note: this is the European Central Bank's rate on the marginal lending facility, which offers overnight credit to banks in the euro area

Commercial bank prime lending rate:

3.55% (31 December 2012 est.)

country comparison to the world: 172

3.81% (31 December 2011 est.)

Stock of narrow money:

$122.2 billion (31 December 2012 est.)

country comparison to the world: 30

$118.3 billion (31 December 2011 est.)

note: see entry for the European Union for money supply in the euro area; the European Central Bank (ECB) controls monetary policy for the 17 members of the Economic and Monetary Union (EMU); individual members of the EMU do not control the quantity of money circulating within their own borders

Stock of broad money:

$291.1 billion (31 December 2011 est.)

country comparison to the world: 33

$260 billion (31 December 2010 est.)

Stock of domestic credit:

$432.8 billion (31 December 2012 est.)

country comparison to the world: 28

$456.8 billion (31 December 2011 est.)

Market value of publicly traded shares:

$35.36 billion (31 December 2011)

country comparison to the world: 57

$33.72 billion (31 December 2010)

$29.88 billion (31 December 2009)

Agriculture - products:

barley, potatoes, wheat; beef, dairy products

Industries:

pharmaceuticals, chemicals, computer hardware and software, food products, beverages and brewing; medical devices

Industrial production growth rate:

-0.1% (2012 est.)

country comparison to the world: 136

Current account balance:

$3.5 billion (2012 est.)

country comparison to the world: 32

$2.484 billion (2011 est.)

Exports:

$119 billion (2012 est.)

country comparison to the world: 36

$126.7 billion (2011 est.)

Exports - commodities:

machinery and equipment, computers, chemicals, medical devices, pharmaceuticals; food products, animal products

Exports - partners:

US 18%, UK 17.4%, Belgium 15.6%, Germany 8.4%, Switzerland 5.8%, France 5% (2012)

Imports:
$64.32 billion (2012 est.)
country comparison to the world: 47
$67.11 billion (2011 est.)

Imports - commodities:
data processing equipment, other machinery and equipment, chemicals, petroleum and petroleum products, textiles, clothing

Imports - partners:
UK 40%, US 13.2%, Germany 7.6%, Netherlands 5.6% (2012)

Reserves of foreign exchange and gold:
$1.707 billion (31 December 2012 est.)
country comparison to the world: 126
$1.703 billion (31 December 2011 est.)

Debt - external:
$2.163 trillion (31 December 2012)
country comparison to the world: 11
$2.213 trillion (31 December 2011)

Stock of direct foreign investment - at home:
$276.4 billion (31 December 2012 est.)
country comparison to the world: 19
$243.5 billion (31 December 2011 est.)

Stock of direct foreign investment - abroad:
$347 billion (31 December 2012 est.)
country comparison to the world: 17
$324.2 billion (31 December 2011 est.)

Exchange rates:
euros (EUR) per US dollar:
0.7778 (2012 est.)
0.7185 (2011 est.)

0.755 (2010 est.)
0.7198 (2009 est.)
0.6827 (2008 est.)

Fiscal year:
calendar year

Chapter 6: Energy

Electricity - production:
26.35 billion kWh (2011 est.)
country comparison to the world: 69

Electricity - consumption:
26.1 billion kWh (2011 est.)
country comparison to the world: 67

Electricity - exports:
242 million kWh (2011 est.)
country comparison to the world: 66

Electricity - imports:
732 million kWh (2011 est.)
country comparison to the world: 69

Electricity - installed generating capacity:
7.401 million kW (2009 est.)
country comparison to the world: 65

Electricity - from fossil fuels:
75.3% of total installed capacity (2009 est.)
country comparison to the world: 99

Electricity - from nuclear fuels:
0% of total installed capacity (2009 est.)
country comparison to the world: 82

Electricity - from hydroelectric plants:
3.2% of total installed capacity (2009 est.)
country comparison to the world: 129

Electricity - from other renewable sources:
17.5% of total installed capacity (2009 est.)
country comparison to the world: 8

Crude oil - production:
0 bbl/day (2011 est.)

country comparison to the world: 129

Crude oil - exports:

0 bbl/day (2009 est.)

country comparison to the world: 105

Crude oil - imports:

53,560 bbl/day (2009 est.)

country comparison to the world: 56

Crude oil - proved reserves:

0 bbl (1 January 2012 est.)

country comparison to the world: 127

Refined petroleum products - production:

55,340 bbl/day (2009 est.)

country comparison to the world: 84

Refined petroleum products - consumption:

144,000 bbl/day (2011 est.)

country comparison to the world: 70

Refined petroleum products - exports:

17,480 bbl/day (2010 est.)

country comparison to the world: 76

Refined petroleum products - imports:

166,000 bbl/day (2009 est.)

country comparison to the world: 34

Natural gas - production:

346 million cu m (2011 est.)

country comparison to the world: 73

Natural gas - consumption:

4.981 billion cu m (2011 est.)

country comparison to the world: 60

Natural gas - exports:

0 cu m (2011 est.)

country comparison to the world: 92

Natural gas - imports:

4.633 billion cu m (2011 est.)

country comparison to the world: 35

Natural gas - proved reserves:

9.911 billion cu m (1 January 2012 est.)

country comparison to the world: 81

Carbon dioxide emissions from consumption of energy:

40.48 million Mt (2010 est.)

country comparison to the world: 69

Chapter 7: Communications

Telephones - main lines in use:
2.047 million (2011)
country comparison to the world: 57

Telephones - mobile cellular:
4.906 million (2011)
country comparison to the world: 106

Telephone system:
general assessment: modern digital system using cable and microwave radio relay
domestic: system privatized but dominated by former state monopoly operator; increasing levels of broadband access particularly in urban areas
international: country code - 353; landing point for the Hibernia-Atlantic submarine cable with links to the US, Canada, and UK; satellite earth station - 1 Intelsat (Atlantic Ocean) (2011)

Broadcast media:
publicly owned broadcaster Radio Telefis Eireann (RTE) operates 2 TV stations; commercial TV stations are available; about 75% of households utilize multi-channel satellite and TV services that provide access to a wide range of stations; RTE operates 4 national radio stations and has launched digital audio broadcasts on several stations; a number of commercial broadcast stations operate at the national, regional, and local levels (2007)

Internet country code:
.ie

Internet hosts:
1.387 million (2012)
country comparison to the world: 40

Internet users:
3.042 million (2009)
country comparison to the world: 67

Chapter 8: Transportation

Airports:
    39 (2012)
    country comparison to the world: 107

Airports - with paved runways:
    total: 16
    over 3,047 m: 1
    2,438 to 3,047 m: 1
    1,524 to 2,437 m: 4
    914 to 1,523 m: 5
    under 914 m: 5 (2012)

Airports - with unpaved runways:
    total: 23
    914 to 1,523 m: 2
    under 914 m: 21 (2012)

Pipelines:
    gas 2,147 km (2013)

Railways:
    total: 3,237 km
    country comparison to the world: 54
    broad gauge: 1,872 km 1.600-m gauge (37 km electrified)
    narrow gauge: 1,365 km 0.914-m gauge (operated by the Irish Peat Board to transport peat to power stations and briquetting plants) (2008)

Roadways:
    total: 96,036 km
    country comparison to the world: 45
    paved: 96,036 km (includes 1,224 km of expressways) (2010)

Waterways:
    956 km (pleasure craft only) (2010)
    country comparison to the world: 68

Merchant marine:
   total: 31
   country comparison to the world: 83
   by type: cargo 28, chemical tanker 2, container 1
   foreign-owned: 5 (France 2, Spain 1, US 2)
   registered in other countries: 33 (Bahamas 3, Bermuda 1, Cambodia 1, Cyprus 3, Isle of Man 1, Kazakhstan 1, Malta 4, Marshall Islands 6, Netherlands 8, Panama 1, Russia 1, Slovakia 1, Sweden 1, UK 1) (2010)

Ports and terminals:
   Cork, Dublin, Shannon Foynes, Waterford

Chapter 9: Military

Military branches:

Irish Defense Forces (Oglaigh na h-Eireannn), Permanent Defence Force: Army, Naval Service, Air Corps (2012)

Military service age and obligation:

17-25 years of age for male and female voluntary military service (17-27 years of age for the Naval Service); enlistees 16 years of age can be recruited for apprentice specialist positions; 17-35 years of age for the Reserve Defense Forces (RDF); maximum obligation 12 years (5 years IDF, 7 years RDF); EU citizenship or 5-year residence in Ireland required (2012)

Manpower available for military service:

males age 16-49: 1,179,125

females age 16-49: 1,163,728 (2010 est.)

Manpower fit for military service:

males age 16-49: 977,631

females age 16-49: 965,900 (2010 est.)

Manpower reaching militarily significant age annually:

male: 28,564

female: 27,197 (2010 est.)

Military expenditures:

0.9% of GDP (2005 est.)

country comparison to the world: 136

Chapter 10: Transnational Issues

Disputes - international:
>Ireland, Iceland, and the UK dispute Denmark's claim that the Faroe Islands' continental shelf extends beyond 200 nm

Illicit drugs:
>transshipment point for and consumer of hashish from North Africa to the UK and Netherlands and of European-produced synthetic drugs; increasing consumption of South American cocaine; minor transshipment point for heroin and cocaine destined for Western Europe; despite recent legislation, narcotics-related money laundering - using bureaux de change, trusts, and shell companies involving the offshore financial community - remains a concern

Map of Ireland

Other Key Facts™ Titles

Key Facts on Syria

Key Facts on China

Key Facts on Qatar

Key Facts on India

Key Facts on Germany

Key Facts on Argentina

Key Facts on Russia

Key Facts on North Korea

Key Facts on Brazil

Key Facts on Italy

Key Facts on the United Arab Emirates

Key Facts on the European Union

Key Facts on Pakistan

Key Facts on Saudi Arabia

Key Facts on Cyprus

Key Facts on Iran

Key Facts on Afghanistan

Key Facts on Iraq

Key Facts on Indonesia

Key Facts on South Korea

Key Facts on France

Key Facts on the United Kingdom

Key Facts on Egypt

Key Facts on Israel

Key Facts on Mexico

Key Facts on the United States of America

Key Facts on Turkey

Key Facts on South Africa

Key Facts on Greece

Key Facts on Japan

Key Facts on Malaysia

Key Facts on Vietnam

Key Facts on Hong Kong

Key Facts on Jordan

Key Facts on Australia

Key Facts on Venezuela

Key Facts on Canada

Key Facts on Burma (Myanmar)

Key Facts on Myanmar (Burma)

Key Facts on Singapore

Key Facts on the Philippines

All Key Facts™ Titles are Available at www.Amazon.com

THE INTERNATIONALIST®

2013

WWW.INTERNATIONALIST.COM

www.ingramcontent.com/pod-product-compliance
Lightning Source LLC
Chambersburg PA
CBHW070728180526
45167CB00004B/1660